All 66 Books

Know Your Bible

VALUEBOOKS
An Imprint of Barbour Publishing, Inc.

© 2008 by Barbour Publishing, Inc.

ISBN 978-1-60260-015-7

All rights reserved. No part of this publication may be reproduced or transmitted for commercial purposes, except for brief quotations in printed reviews, without written permission of the publisher.

Churches and other noncommercial interests may reproduce portions of this book without the express written permission of Barbour Publishing, provided that the text does not exceed 500 words and that the text is not material quoted from another publisher. When reproducing text from this book, include the following credit line: "From *Know Your Bible*, published by Barbour Publishing, Inc. Used by permission."

All scripture quotations, unless otherwise noted, are taken from the King James Version of the Bible.

Scripture quotations marked NIV are taken from the HOLY BIBLE, NEW INTERNATIONAL VERSION®. NIV®. Copyright © 1973, 1978, 1984 by International Bible Society. Used by permission of Zondervan. All rights reserved.

Scripture quotations marked ASV are taken from the American Standard Version of the Bible.

Published by Value Books, an imprint of Barbour Publishing, Inc., 1810 Barbour Drive, Uhrichsville, Ohio 44683, www.barbourbooks.com

Our mission is to inspire the world with the life-changing message of the Bible.

 Member of the
Evangelical Christian
Publishers Association

Printed in the United States of America.

Contents

INTRODUCTION

Through sixty-six separate books, 1,189 chapters, and hundreds of thousands of words, the Bible shares one extraordinary message: God loves you.

From the first chapter of Genesis, where God creates human beings, through the last chapter of Revelation, where God welcomes anyone to "take the water of life freely" (22:17), the Bible proves God is intimately involved in, familiar with, and concerned about the lives of people. His amazing love is shown in the death of His Son, Jesus Christ, on the cross. That sacrifice for sin allows anyone to be right with God through simple faith in Jesus' work.

These truths are found in the pages of scripture. But sometimes they can be obscured by the vast amount of information the Bible contains. That's why *Know Your Bible* was written.

In this little book, you'll find brief surveys of all sixty-six Bible books. Each summarizes what that book is about—always within the context of God's love and concern for people. Every entry follows this outline:

• AUTHOR: who wrote the book, according to the Bible itself or ancient tradition.

• DATE: when the book was written or the time the book covers.

• IN TEN WORDS OR LESS: a "nutshell" glance at the book's key theme.

• DETAILS, PLEASE: a synopsis of the key people, events, and messages covered in the book.

- QUOTABLE: one, two, or several key verses from the book.

- UNIQUE AND UNUSUAL: facts—some serious, some less so—that make the book stand out.

- SO WHAT? an inspirational or devotional thought for each book.

Your Bible is certainly worth knowing. Use this book to begin a journey of discovery that could truly change your life!

GENESIS

AUTHOR

Not stated but traditionally attributed to Moses.

DATE

Moses lived around the 1400s BC, but the events of Genesis date to the very beginning of time.

IN TEN WORDS OR LESS

God creates the world and chooses a special people.

DETAILS, PLEASE

The Bible's first book never explains God; it simply assumes His existence: "In the beginning, God..." (1:1). Chapters 1 and 2 describe how God created the universe and everything in it simply by speaking: "God said...and it was so" (1:6–7, 9, 11, 14–15). Humans, however, received special handling, as "God formed man of the dust of the ground, and breathed into his nostrils the breath of life" (2:7), and woman was crafted from a rib of man. Those first two people, Adam and Eve, live in perfection but ruined paradise by disobeying God at the urging of a "subtil" (crafty, 3:1) serpent. Sin throws humans into a moral freefall as the world's first child—Cain—murders his brother Abel. People become so bad that God decides to flood the entire planet, saving only the righteous Noah, his family, and an ark (boat) full of animals. After the earth repopulates, God chooses a man named Abram as patriarch of a specially blessed people, later called "Israel" after an alternative name of Abram's grandson Jacob. Genesis ends with Jacob's son Joseph, by a miraculous chain of events, ruling in Egypt—setting up the events of the following book of Exodus.

QUOTABLE

God said, Let there be light: and there was light. (1:3)

The LORD said unto Cain, Where is Abel thy brother? And he said, I know not: Am I my brother's keeper? (4:9)

Noah found grace in the eyes of the LORD. (6:8)

He [Abram] believed in the LORD; and he counted it to him for righteousness. (15:6)

UNIQUE AND UNUSUAL

Genesis quickly introduces the concept of one God in multiple persons, a concept later called the Trinity: "God said, Let us make man in our image, after our likeness" (1:26, emphasis added). Also early on, God gives a hint of Jesus' future suffering and victory when He curses the serpent for deceiving Eve: "I will put enmity between thee and the woman, and between thy seed and her seed; it shall bruise thy head, and thou shalt bruise his heel" (3:15).

SO WHAT?

Genesis answers the great question "Where did I come from?" Knowing the answer can give us meaning in a world that's otherwise hard to figure out.

Exodus

Author

Not stated but traditionally attributed to Moses. In Exodus 34:27 God tells Moses, "Write thou these words," and Jesus, in Mark 12:26, quotes from Exodus as "the book of Moses."

Date

Approximately the mid-1400s BC.

In Ten Words or Less

God delivers His people, the Israelites, from slavery in Egypt.

Details, Please

The Israelites prosper in Egypt, having settled there at the invitation of Abraham's great-grandson Joseph, who entered the country as a slave and rose to second in command. When Joseph dies, a new pharaoh sees the burgeoning family as a threat—and makes the people his slaves. God hears the Israelites' groaning, remembering "his covenant with Abraham, with Isaac, and with Jacob" (2:24) and raising up Moses as their deliverer. God speaks through a burning bush, and Moses reluctantly agrees to demand the Israelites' release from Pharaoh. To break Pharaoh's will, God sends ten plagues on Egypt, ending with the death of every firstborn child—except those of the Israelites. They put sacrificial blood on their doorposts, causing the Lord to "pass over" (12:13) their homes. Pharaoh finally allows the Israelites to leave the country (the "Exodus"), and God parts the Red Sea for the people, who are being pursued by Egyptian soldiers. At Mount Sinai, God delivers the Ten Commandments, rules for worship, and laws to change the family into a nation. When Moses delays on the mountain, the people begin worshipping a golden calf, bringing a plague upon themselves. Moses returns to restore order, and Exodus ends with the people continuing their journey to the "promised land" of Canaan, following God's "pillar of cloud" by day and "pillar of fire" by night.

QUOTABLE

God said unto Moses, I AM THAT I AM: and he said, Thus shalt thou say unto the children of Israel, I AM hath sent me unto you. (3:14)

Thus saith the LORD, Let my people go. (8:1)

When I see the blood, I will pass over you. (12:13)

Thou shalt have no other gods before me. (20:3)

UNIQUE AND UNUSUAL

God told the Israelites to celebrate the "Passover" with a special meal of bread made without yeast (12:14–15). Three thousand years later, Jewish people still commemorate the event.

SO WHAT?

The story of redemption is on clear display in Exodus as God rescues His people from their slavery in Egypt. In the same way, Jesus breaks our bonds of sin (Hebrews 2:14–15).

LEVITICUS

AUTHOR

Not stated but traditionally attributed to Moses.

DATE

Approximately the mid-1400s BC.

IN TEN WORDS OR LESS

A holy God explains how to worship Him.

DETAILS, PLEASE

Leviticus, meaning "about the Levites," describes how that family line should lead the Israelites in worship. The book provides ceremonial laws as opposed to the moral laws of Exodus, describing offerings to God, dietary restrictions, and purification rites. Special holy days—including the Sabbath, Passover, and Day of Atonement (Yom Kippur)—are commanded. The family of Aaron, Moses' brother, is ordained as Israel's formal priesthood. Leviticus lists several blessings for obedience and many more punishments for disobedience.

QUOTABLE

Ye shall be holy; for I [God] am holy. (11:44)

The life of the flesh is in the blood. . .it is the blood that maketh an atonement for the soul. (17:11)

UNIQUE AND UNUSUAL

Leviticus's blood sacrifices are contrasted with Jesus' death on the cross by the writer of Hebrews: "Who needeth not daily, as those high priests, to offer up sacrifice. . .for this he did once, when he offered up himself" (7:27).

SO WHAT?

Though we don't live under the rules of Leviticus, we still serve a holy God—and should treat Him as such.

Numbers

Author

Not stated but traditionally attributed to Moses.

Date

Approximately 1400 BC.

In Ten Words or Less

Faithless Israelites wander forty years in the wilderness of Sinai.

Details, Please

Numbers begins with a census—hence the book's name. Fourteen months after the Israelites escape Egypt, they number 603,550 men, not including the Levites. This mass of people, the newly formed nation of Israel, begins a march of approximately two hundred miles to the "promised land" of Canaan—a journey that will take decades to complete. The delay is God's punishment of the people, who complain about food and water, rebel against Moses, and hesitate to enter Canaan because of powerful people already living there. God decrees that this entire generation will die in the wilderness, leaving the Promised Land to a new generation of more obedient Israelites.

Quotable

The LORD is longsuffering, and of great mercy, forgiving iniquity and transgression. (14:18)

Unique and Unusual

Even Moses misses out on the Promised Land, punishment for disobeying God by striking, rather than speaking to, a rock from which water would miraculously appear (20:1–13).

So What?

God hates sin and punishes it. We can be thankful that Jesus took that punishment for us.

DEUTERONOMY

AUTHOR

Traditionally attributed to Moses, an idea supported by Deuteronomy 31:9: "Moses wrote this law, and delivered it unto the priests. . .and unto all the elders of Israel." Chapter 34, recording Moses' death, was probably written by his successor, Joshua.

DATE

Approximately 1400 BC.

IN TEN WORDS OR LESS

Moses reminds the Israelites of their history and God's laws.

DETAILS, PLEASE

With a name meaning "second law," Deuteronomy records Moses' final words as the Israelites prepare to enter the Promised Land. Forty years have passed since God handed down His laws on Mount Sinai, and the entire generation that experienced that momentous event has died. So Moses reminds the new generation both of God's commands and of their national history as they ready their entry into Canaan. The invasion will occur under Joshua, as Moses will only *see* the Promised Land from Mount Nebo. "So Moses the servant of the LORD died there. . . . And he [God] buried him in a valley in the land of Moab. . .but no man knoweth of his sepulchre unto this day" (34:5–6). Moses was 120 years old.

QUOTABLE

Hear, O Israel: The LORD our God is one LORD. (6:4)

Thou shalt love the LORD thy God with all thine heart, and with all thy soul, and with all thy might. (6:5)

The LORD thy God is a jealous God among you. (6:15)

Unique and Unusual

The New Testament quotes from Deuteronomy dozens of times, including three from the story of Jesus' temptation in the wilderness in Matthew 4:1–11. The Lord defeated Satan by restating Deuteronomy 8:3 ("Man shall not live by bread alone, but by every word that proceedeth out of the mouth of God"); 6:16 ("Thou shalt not tempt the Lord thy God"); and 6:13 ("Thou shalt worship the Lord thy God, and him only shalt thou serve").

The Ten Commandments, most commonly found in Exodus 20, are restated in full in Deuteronomy 5.

So What?

Deuteronomy makes clear that God's rules and expectations aren't meant to limit and frustrate us but instead to benefit us: "Hear therefore, O Israel, and observe to do it; that it may be well with thee, and that ye may increase mightily, as the LORD God of thy fathers hath promised thee, in the land that floweth with milk and honey" (6:3).

JOSHUA

AUTHOR

Traditionally attributed to Joshua himself, except for the final five verses (24:29–33), which describe Joshua's death and legacy.

DATE

Approximately 1375 BC.

IN TEN WORDS OR LESS

The Israelites capture and settle the promised land of Canaan.

DETAILS, PLEASE

With Moses and an entire generation of disobedient Israelites dead, God tells Joshua to lead the people into Canaan, their promised land. In Jericho, the first major obstacle, the prostitute Rahab helps Israelite spies and earns protection from the destruction of the city: God knocks its walls flat as Joshua's army marches outside, blowing trumpets and shouting. Joshua leads a successful military campaign to clear idol-worshipping people—Hittites, Amorites, Canaanites, Perizzites, Hivites, and Jebusites—from the land. At one point, God answers Joshua's prayer to make the sun stand still, allowing more time to complete a battle (10:1–15). Major cities subdued, Joshua divides the land among the twelve tribes of Israel, reminding the people to stay true to the God who led them home: "Now therefore put away. . .the strange gods which are among you, and incline your heart unto the LORD God of Israel" (24:23).

QUOTABLE

Be strong and of a good courage; be not afraid, neither be thou dismayed: for the LORD thy God is with thee whithersoever thou goest. (1:9)

One man of you shall chase a thousand: for the LORD your God, he it is that fighteth for you, as he hath promised you. (23:10)

Choose you this day whom ye will serve. . .as for me and my house, we will serve the LORD. (24:15)

UNIQUE AND UNUSUAL

Joshua is one of few major Bible characters who seemed to do everything right—he was a strong leader, completely committed to God, who never fell into recorded sin or disobedience. Only one mistake mars his record: Joshua's experience with the Gibeonites, one of the local groups he should have destroyed. Fearing for their lives, they appeared before Joshua dressed in old clothes, carrying dry, moldy bread, claiming they had come from a faraway land. Joshua and the Israelite leaders "asked not counsel at the mouth of the LORD" (9:14) and agreed to a peace treaty. When Joshua learned the truth, he honored his agreement with the Gibeonites—but made them slaves.

SO WHAT?

Joshua shows over and over how God blesses His people. The Promised Land was His gift to them, as were the military victories that He engineered.

JUDGES

AUTHOR

Unknown; some suggest the prophet Samuel.

DATE

Written approximately 1050 BC, covering events that occurred as far back as 1375 BC.

IN TEN WORDS OR LESS

Israel goes through cycles of sin, suffering, and salvation.

DETAILS, PLEASE

After Joshua's death, the Israelites lose momentum in driving pagan people out of the Promised Land. "The children of Benjamin did not drive out the Jebusites that inhabited Jerusalem" (1:21) is a statement characteristic of many tribes, which allow idol worshippers to stay in their midst—with tragic results. "Ye have not obeyed my voice" God says to His people. "They shall be as thorns in your sides, and their gods shall be a snare unto you" (2:2–3). That's exactly what happens, as the Israelites begin a cycle of worshipping idols, suffering punishment by attackers, crying to God for help, and receiving God's aid in the form of a human judge (or "deliverer") who restores order. Lesser-known judges include Othniel, Ehud, Tola, Jair, and Jephthah, while more familiar figures are Deborah, the only female judge, who led a military victory against the Canaanites; Gideon, who tested God's will with a fleece and defeated the armies of Midian; and the amazingly strong Samson, who defeated the Philistines. Samson's great weakness—his love for unsavory women such as Delilah—led to his downfall and death in a Philistine temple.

QUOTABLE

They forsook the LORD God of their fathers, which brought them out of the land of Egypt, and followed other gods, of the gods of the people that were round about them. (2:12)

The LORD raised up judges, which delivered them out of the hand of those that spoiled them. (2:16)

The LORD said unto Gideon, The people that are with thee are too many for me to give the Midianites into their hands, lest Israel vaunt themselves against me, saying, Mine own hand hath saved me. (7:2)

UNIQUE AND UNUSUAL

Several judges had unusual families by today's standards: Jair had thirty sons (10:4), Abdon had forty sons (12:14), and Ibzan had thirty sons and thirty daughters (12:9). Jephthah had only one child, a daughter, whom he foolishly vowed to sacrifice to God in exchange for a military victory (11:30–40).

SO WHAT?

The ancient Israelites got into trouble when they "did that which was right in [their] own eyes" (17:6; 21:25) rather than what God wanted them to do. Don't make the same mistake yourself!

Ruth

Author

Not stated; some suggest Samuel.

Date

Ruth, the great-grandmother of King David (who reigned approximately 1010–970 BC), probably lived around 1100 BC.

In Ten Words or Less

Loyal daughter-in-law pictures God's faithfulness, love, and care.

Details, Please

Ruth, a Gentile woman, marries into a Jewish family. When all of the men of the family die, Ruth shows loyalty to her mother-in-law, Naomi, staying with her and scavenging food to keep them alive. As Ruth gleans barley in a field of the wealthy Boaz, he takes an interest in her and orders his workers to watch over her. Naomi recognizes Boaz as her late husband's relative and encourages Ruth to pursue him as a "kinsman redeemer," one who weds a relative's widow to continue a family line. Boaz marries Ruth, starting a prominent family.

Quotable

Whither thou goest, I will go; and where thou lodgest, I will lodge: thy people shall be my people, and thy God my God. (1:16)

Unique and Unusual

Ruth, from the pagan land of Moab, married a Jewish man and became the great-grandmother of Israel's greatest king, David—and an ancestor of Jesus Christ.

So What?

We can trust God to provide what we need, when we need it—and to work out our lives in ways that are better than we ever imagined.

1 Samuel

Author

Not stated. Samuel himself was likely involved, though some of the history of 1 Samuel occurs after the prophet's death.

Date

Approximately 1100–1000 BC.

In Ten Words or Less

Israel's twelve tribes unite under a king.

Details, Please

An infertile woman, Hannah, begs God for a son, promising to return him to the Lord's service. Samuel is born and soon sent to the temple to serve under the aging priest, Eli. Upon Eli's death, Samuel serves as judge, or deliverer, of Israel, subduing the nation's fearsome enemy, the Philistines. As Samuel ages, Israel's tribal leaders reject his sinful sons and ask for a king. Samuel warns that a king will tax the people and force them into service, but they insist and God tells Samuel to anoint the notably tall and handsome Saul as Israel's first ruler. King Saul starts well but begins making poor choices—and when he offers a sacrifice to God, a job reserved for priests, Samuel tells Saul that he will be replaced. Saul's successor will be a shepherd named David, who with God's help kills a giant Philistine warrior named Goliath and becomes Israel's hero. The jealous king seeks to kill David, who runs for his life. David rejects opportunities to kill Saul himself, saying, "I would not stretch forth mine hand against the LORD's anointed" (26:23). At the end of 1 Samuel, Saul dies battling the Philistines, making way for David to become king.

Quotable

The LORD said unto Samuel. . .they have not rejected thee, but they have rejected me, that I should not reign over them. (8:7)

Behold, to obey is better than sacrifice, and to hearken than the fat of rams. (15:22)

Then said David to the Philistine [Goliath], Thou comest to me with a sword, and with a spear, and with a shield: but I come to thee in the name of the LORD of hosts, the God of the armies of Israel, whom thou hast defied. (17:45)

UNIQUE AND UNUSUAL

The future King Saul is a donkey herder (9:5) who tries to hide from his own coronation (10:21–22). As king, Saul breaks his own law by asking a medium to call up the spirit of the dead Samuel (chapter 28).

SO WHAT?

Selfish choices—such as the Israelites' request for a king and Saul's decision to offer a sacrifice he had no business making—can have heavy, even tragic, consequences.

2 SAMUEL

AUTHOR

Unknown but not Samuel—since the events of the book take place after his death. Some suggest Abiathar the priest (15:35).

DATE

Approximately 1010–970 BC, the reign of King David.

IN TEN WORDS OR LESS

David becomes Israel's greatest king—but with major flaws.

DETAILS, PLEASE

When King Saul dies, David is made king by the southern Jewish tribe of Judah. Seven years later, after the death of Saul's son Ish-bosheth, king of the northern tribes, David becomes ruler of all Israel. Capturing Jerusalem from the Jebusites, David creates a new capital for his unified nation, and God promises David, "Your throne will be established forever" (7:16 NIV). Military victories make Israel strong, but when David stays home from battle one spring, he commits adultery with a beautiful neighbor, Bathsheba. Then he has her husband—one of his soldiers—murdered. The prophet Nathan confronts David with a story of a rich man who steals a poor man's sheep. David is furious until Nathan announces, "Thou art the man" (12:7). Chastened, David repents and God forgives his sins—but their consequences will affect David powerfully. The baby conceived in the tryst dies, and David's family begins to splinter apart. One of David's sons, Amnon, rapes his half sister, and a second son, Absalom—full brother to the violated girl—kills Amnon in revenge. Absalom then conspires to steal the kingdom from David, causing his father to flee for his life. When Absalom dies in battle with David's men, David grieves so deeply that he offends his soldiers. Ultimately, David returns to Jerusalem to reassert his kingship. He also raises another son born to Bathsheba—Solomon.

QUOTABLE

How are the mighty fallen in the midst of the battle! (1:25)

Who am I, O Lord GOD? and what is my house, that thou hast brought me hitherto? (7:18)

O my son Absalom, my son, my son Absalom! would God I had died for thee, O Absalom, my son, my son! (18:33)

UNIQUE AND UNUSUAL

David's nephew killed a Philistine "of great stature, that had on every hand six fingers, and on every foot six toes" (21:20). David's top soldier, Adino, once killed 800 men single-handedly (23:8).

SO WHAT?

King David's story highlights the vital importance of the choices we make. Who would have guessed that such a great man could fall into such terrible sin?

1 Kings

Author

Not stated and unknown; one early tradition claimed Jeremiah wrote 1 and 2 Kings.

Date

Covering events from about 970 to 850 BC, 1 Kings was probably written sometime after the Babylonian destruction of Jerusalem in 586 BC.

In Ten Words or Less

Israel divides into rival northern and southern nations.

Details, Please

King David, in declining health, names Solomon, his son with Bathsheba, successor. After David's death, God speaks to Solomon in a dream, offering him anything he'd like—and Solomon chooses wisdom. God gives Solomon great wisdom, along with much power and wealth. The new king soon builds God a permanent temple in Jerusalem, and the Lord visits Solomon again to promise blessings for obedience and trouble for disobedience. Sadly, Solomon's wisdom fails him, as he marries seven hundred women, many of them foreigners who turn his heart to idols. When Solomon dies, his son Rehoboam foolishly antagonizes the people of Israel, and ten northern tribes form their own nation under Jeroboam, a former official of Solomon's. Two southern tribes continue under Solomon's line in a nation called Judah. Jeroboam begins badly, initiating idol worship in the north; many wicked rulers follow. Judah will also have many poor leaders, though occasional kings, such as Asa and Jehoshaphat, follow the Lord. 1 Kings introduces the prophet Elijah, who confronts the evil King Ahab and Queen Jezebel of Israel regarding their worship of the false god Baal. In God's power, Elijah defeats 450 false prophets in a dramatic contest on Mount Carmel.

QUOTABLE

David drew nigh that he should die; and he charged Solomon his son, saying, I go the way of all the earth: be thou strong therefore, and shew thyself a man. (2:1–2)

Give therefore thy servant an understanding heart to judge thy people, that I may discern between good and bad: for who is able to judge this thy so great a people? (3:9)

Hear me, O LORD, hear me, that this people may know that thou art the LORD God, and that thou hast turned their heart back again. (18:37)

UNIQUE AND UNUSUAL

Scholars say 1 and 2 Kings were originally a single volume and were split in half to allow for copying onto normal-sized scrolls.

SO WHAT?

Solomon's example provides a strong warning: Even the most blessed person can drift from God and make big mistakes.

2 KINGS

AUTHOR

Not stated and unknown; one early tradition claimed Jeremiah wrote 1 and 2 Kings.

DATE

Covering about three hundred years from the 800s BC on, 2 Kings was probably written sometime after the Babylonian destruction of Jerusalem in 586 BC.

IN TEN WORDS OR LESS

Both Jewish nations are destroyed for their disobedience to God.

DETAILS, PLEASE

The story of 1 Kings continues, with more bad rulers, a handful of good ones, some familiar prophets, and the ultimate loss of the two Jewish nations. Early in 2 Kings, Elijah becomes the second man (after Enoch in Genesis 5:24) to go straight to heaven without dying. His successor, Elisha, performs many miracles and shares God's word with the "average people" of Israel. The northern kingdom's rulers are entirely wicked, and Israel, under its last king, Hoshea, is "carried. . .away into Assyria" (17:6) in 722 BC. Judah, with occasional good kings such as Hezekiah and Josiah, lasts a few years longer—but in 586 BC the southern kingdom's capital of Jerusalem "was broken up" (25:4) by Babylonian armies under King Nebuchadnezzar. Besides taking everything valuable from the temple and the Jewish king's palace, the Babylonians also "carried away all Jerusalem, and all the princes, and all the mighty men of valour, even ten thousand captives, and all the craftsmen and smiths" (24:14). Ending on a slight up note, 2 Kings describes a new king of Babylon, Evil-merodach, showing kindness to Jehoiachin, the last real king of Judah, by giving him a place of honor in the Babylonian court.

QUOTABLE

Behold, there appeared a chariot of fire, and horses of fire, and parted them both asunder; and Elijah went up by a whirlwind into heaven. (2:11)

The LORD rejected all the seed of Israel, and afflicted them, and delivered them into the hand of spoilers, until he had cast them out of his sight. (17:20)

So Judah was carried away out of their land. (25:21)

UNIQUE AND UNUSUAL

Isaiah, who wrote a long prophecy that appears later in the Old Testament, is prominent in 2 Kings 19. One of Judah's best kings, Josiah, was only eight years old when he took the throne (22:1).

SO WHAT?

Both Israel and Judah found that there were terrible consequences to sin. Even bad examples can be helpful if we decide not to do the things that bring us trouble.

1 Chronicles

Author

Not stated but traditionally attributed to Ezra the priest.

Date

Covers the history of Israel from about 1010 BC (the death of King Saul) to about 970 BC (the death of King David).

In Ten Words or Less

King David's reign is detailed and analyzed.

Details, Please

1 Chronicles provides a history of Israel, going as far back as Adam. By the eleventh chapter, the story turns to Israel's greatest king, David, with special emphasis on his leadership of national worship. Another important focus is on God's promise that David would have an eternal kingly line through his descendant Jesus Christ.

Quotable

I will settle him in mine house and in my kingdom for ever: and his throne shall be established for evermore. (17:14)

Unique and Unusual

1 Chronicles covers much of the same information as 2 Samuel, but without some of the seedier aspects of David's life—such as his adultery with Bathsheba and the engineered killing of her husband, Uriah.

So What?

The positive spin of 1 Chronicles was designed to remind the Jews that despite their punishment for sin, they were still God's special people. When God makes a promise, He keeps it.

2 Chronicles

Author

Not stated but traditionally attributed to Ezra the priest.

Date

Covers Israelite history from about 970 BC (the accession of King Solomon) to the 500s BC (when exiled Jews returned to Jerusalem).

In Ten Words or Less

The history of Israel from Solomon to division to destruction.

Details, Please

David's son Solomon is made king, builds the temple, and becomes one of the most prominent rulers ever. But when he dies, the Jewish nation divides. In the remainder of 2 Chronicles, the various kings of the relatively godlier southern nation of Judah are profiled right down to the destruction of Jerusalem by the Babylonians. The book ends with the Persian king Cyrus allowing Jews to rebuild the devastated temple.

Quotable

O LORD God of Israel, there is no God like thee in the heaven, nor in the earth; which keepest covenant, and shewest mercy unto thy servants, that walk before thee with all their hearts. (6:14)

Unique and Unusual

Continuing the positive spin of 1 Chronicles (the two books were originally one), 2 Chronicles ends with two verses that exactly repeat the first three verses of Ezra.

So What?

God's punishment isn't intended to hurt people but to bring them back to Him.

Ezra

Author

Not stated but traditionally attributed to Ezra the priest (7:11).

Date

Approximately 530 BC to the mid-400s BC.

In Ten Words or Less

Spiritual renewal begins after the Jews return from exile.

Details, Please

About a half century after Babylonians sacked Jerusalem and carried Jews into captivity, Persia is the new world power. King Cyrus allows a group of exiles to return to Judah to rebuild the temple. Some 42,000 people return and resettle the land. About seventy years later, Ezra is part of a smaller group that also returns. He teaches the law to the people, who have fallen away from God to the point of intermarrying with nearby pagan nations, something that was strictly forbidden by Moses (Deuteronomy 7:1–3).

Quotable

Ezra had prepared his heart to seek the law of the LORD, and to do it, and to teach in Israel statutes and judgments. (7:10)

Unique and Unusual

Though God has said, "I hate divorce" (Malachi 2:16 NIV), Ezra urged Jewish men to separate from their foreign wives.

So What?

In Ezra, God shows His willingness to offer a second chance—allowing a nation that had been punished for disobedience to have a fresh start. Guess what? He's still in the second-chance business.

NEHEMIAH

AUTHOR

"The words of Nehemiah" (1:1), though Jewish tradition says those words were put on paper by Ezra.

DATE

Approximately 445 BC.

IN TEN WORDS OR LESS

Returning Jewish exiles rebuild the broken walls of Jerusalem.

DETAILS, PLEASE

Nehemiah serves as "the king's cupbearer" (1:11) in Shushan, Persia. As a Jew, he's disturbed to learn that even though exiles have been back in Judah for nearly a hundred years, they have not rebuilt the city's walls, devastated by the Babylonians in 586 BC. Nehemiah asks and receives the king's permission to return to Jerusalem, where he leads a team of builders—against much pagan opposition—in reconstructing the walls in only fifty-two days. The quick work on the project shocks the Jews' enemies, who "perceived that this work was wrought of our God" (6:16).

QUOTABLE

Think upon me, my God, for good, according to all that I have done for this people. (5:19)

UNIQUE AND UNUSUAL

Indignant over some fellow Jews' intermarriage with pagans, Nehemiah "cursed them, and smote certain of them, and plucked off their hair" (13:25).

SO WHAT?

Nehemiah's success in rebuilding Jerusalem's walls provides many leadership principles for today—especially his consistent focus on prayer.

ESTHER

AUTHOR

Not stated but perhaps Ezra or Nehemiah.

DATE

Approximately 486–465 BC, during the reign of King Ahasuerus of Persia. Esther became queen around 479 BC.

IN TEN WORDS OR LESS

Beautiful Jewish girl becomes queen, saves fellow Jews from slaughter.

DETAILS, PLEASE

In a nationwide beauty contest, young Esther becomes queen of Persia without revealing her Jewish heritage. When a royal official plots to kill every Jew in the country, Esther risks her own life to request the king's protection. The king, pleased with Esther, is shocked by his official's plan and has the man hanged—while decreeing that the Jews should defend themselves against the planned slaughter. Esther's people prevail and commemorate the event with a holiday called Purim.

QUOTABLE

Esther obtained favour in the sight of all them that looked upon her. (2:15)

Who knoweth whether thou art come to the kingdom for such a time as this? (4:14)

UNIQUE AND UNUSUAL

God's name is never mentioned in the book of Esther. Neither is prayer, though Esther asks her fellow Jews to fast for her before she approaches the king (4:16).

SO WHAT?

When we find ourselves in bad situations, it may be for the same reason Esther did—to accomplish something good.

Job

Author

Not stated.

Date

Unclear, but many believe Job is one of the oldest stories in the Bible, perhaps from approximately 2000 BC.

In Ten Words or Less

God allows human suffering for His own purposes.

Details, Please

Head of a large family, Job is a wealthy farmer from a place called Uz. He's "perfect and upright" (1:1)—so much so, that God calls Satan's attention to him. The devil, unimpressed, asks and receives God's permission to attack Job's possessions—and wipes out thousands of sheep, camels, oxen, donkeys, and worst of all, Job's ten children. Despite Satan's attack, Job keeps his faith. Satan then receives God's permission to attack Job's health—but in spite of terrible physical suffering, Job refuses to "curse God, and die" as his wife suggests (2:9). Before long, though, Job begins to question why God would allow him—a good man—to suffer so severely. Job's suffering is worsened by the arrival of four "friends" who begin to accuse him of causing his own trouble by secret sin. "Is not thy wickedness great?" asks Eliphaz the Temanite (22:5). In the end, God Himself speaks, vindicating Job before his friends and also addressing the overarching issue of human suffering. God doesn't explain Job's suffering but asks a series of questions that shows His vast knowledge—implying that Job should simply trust God's way. And Job does, telling God, "I know that thou canst do every thing" (42:2). By story's end, God has restored Job's health, possessions, and family, giving him ten more children.

Quotable

Naked came I out of my mother's womb, and naked shall I return thither: the LORD gave, and the LORD hath taken away; blessed be the name of the LORD. (1:21)

Man that is born of a woman is of few days and full of trouble. (14:1)

Miserable comforters are ye all. (16:2)

I abhor myself, and repent in dust and ashes. (42:6)

Unique and Unusual

The book of Job pictures Satan coming into God's presence (1:6). It also gives a clear Old Testament hint of Jesus' work when Job says, "I know that my redeemer liveth, and that he shall stand at the latter day upon the earth" (19:25).

So What?

Trouble isn't necessarily a sign of sin in a person's life. It may be something God allows to draw us closer to Him.

PSALMS

AUTHORS

Various, with nearly half attributed to King David. Other names noted include Solomon, Moses, Asaph, Ethan, and the sons of Korah. Many psalms don't mention an author.

DATE

Approximately the 1400s BC (Moses' time) through the 500s BC (the time of the Jews' Babylonian exile).

IN TEN WORDS OR LESS

Ancient Jewish songbook showcases prayers, praise—and complaints—to God.

DETAILS, PLEASE

Over several centuries, God led various individuals to compose emotionally charged poems—of which 150 were later compiled into the book we know as Psalms. Many of the psalms are described as "of David," meaning they could be *by*, *for*, or *about* Israel's great king. Highlights of the book include the "shepherd psalm" (23), which describes God as protector and provider; David's cry for forgiveness after his sin with Bathsheba (51); psalms of praise (100 is a powerful example); and the celebration of scripture found in Psalm 119, with almost all of the 176 verses making some reference to God's laws, statutes, commandments, precepts, word, and the like. Some psalms, called "imprecatory," call for God's judgment on enemies (see Psalms 69 and 109, for example). Many psalms express agony of spirit on the writer's part—but nearly every psalm returns to the theme of praise to God. That's the way the book of Psalms ends: "Let every thing that hath breath praise the LORD. Praise ye the LORD" (150:6).

QUOTABLE

O LORD our Lord, how excellent is thy name in all the earth! (8:1)

The LORD is my shepherd; I shall not want. (23:1)

Create in me a clean heart, O God; and renew a right spirit within me. (51:10)

Thy word have I hid in mine heart, that I might not sin against thee. (119:11)

I will lift up mine eyes unto the hills, from whence cometh my help. My help cometh from the LORD. (121:1–2)

Behold, how good and how pleasant it is for brethren to dwell together in unity! (133:1)

UNIQUE AND UNUSUAL

The book of Psalms is the Bible's longest, in terms of both number of chapters (150) and total word count. It contains the longest chapter in the Bible (Psalm 119, with 176 verses) and the shortest (Psalm 117, with 2 verses). Psalm 117 is also the midpoint of the Protestant Bible, with 594 chapters before it and 594 after.

SO WHAT?

The psalms run the gamut of human emotion—which is why so many people turn to them in times of both joy and sadness.

PROVERBS

AUTHORS

Primarily Solomon (1:1), with sections attributed to "the wise" (22:17), Agur (30:1), and King Lemuel (31:1). Little is known of the latter two.

DATE

Solomon reigned approximately 970–930 BC. The staff of King Hezekiah, who lived about two hundred years later, "copied out" the latter chapters of the book we have today (25:1).

IN TEN WORDS OR LESS

Pithy, memorable sayings encourage people to pursue wisdom.

DETAILS, PLEASE

Proverbs doesn't have a story line—it's simply a collection of practical tips for living. Mainly from the pen of King Solomon, the wisest human being ever (in 1 Kings 3:12 God said, "I have given thee a wise and an understanding heart; so that there was none like thee before thee, neither after thee shall any arise like unto thee"), the proverbs speak to issues such as work, money, sex, temptation, drinking, laziness, discipline, and child rearing. Underlying each proverb is the truth that "the fear of the LORD is the beginning of knowledge" (1:7).

QUOTABLE

Trust in the LORD with all thine heart; and lean not unto thine own understanding. (3:5)

Go to the ant, thou sluggard; consider her ways, and be wise. (6:6)

A wise son maketh a glad father: but a foolish son is the heaviness of his mother. (10:1)

As a jewel of gold in a swine's snout, so is a fair woman which is without discretion. (11:22)

He that spareth his rod hateth his son: but he that loveth him chasteneth him betimes. (13:24)

A soft answer turneth away wrath: but grievous words stir up anger. (15:1)

Commit thy works unto the LORD, and thy thoughts shall be established. (16:3)

Even a fool, when he holdeth his peace, is counted wise. (17:28)

The name of the LORD is a strong tower: the righteous runneth into it, and is safe. (18:10)

Wine is a mocker, strong drink is raging. (20:1)

A good name is rather to be chosen than great riches. (22:1)

Answer not a fool according to his folly, lest thou also be like unto him. (26:4)

Faithful are the wounds of a friend. (27:6)

UNIQUE AND UNUSUAL

The final chapter of Proverbs includes a long poem in praise of wives, rather unusual for that time and culture.

SO WHAT?

Wisdom, as Proverbs 4:7 indicates, "is the principal thing. . .with all thy getting get understanding." If you need help with that, just ask God (James 1:5).

ECCLESIASTES

AUTHOR

Not stated but probably Solomon. The author is identified as "the son of David" (1:1) and "king over Israel in Jerusalem" (1:12) and says he had "more wisdom than all they that have been before me" (1:16).

DATE

900s BC.

IN TEN WORDS OR LESS

Apart from God, life is empty and unsatisfying.

DETAILS, PLEASE

A king pursues the things of this world, only to find them unfulfilling. Learning, pleasure, work, laughter—"all is vanity" (1:2). The king also laments the inequities of life: People live, work hard, and die, only to leave their belongings to someone else; the wicked prosper over the righteous; the poor are oppressed. Nevertheless, the king realizes "the conclusion of the whole matter: Fear God, and keep his commandments: for this is the whole duty of man" (12:13).

QUOTABLE

To every thing there is a season, and a time to every purpose under the heaven. (3:1)

Remember now thy Creator in the days of thy youth. (12:1)

UNIQUE AND UNUSUAL

The book's generally negative tone makes some readers wonder if Solomon wrote it late in life, after his hundreds of wives led him to stray from God.

SO WHAT?

Life doesn't always make sense. . .but there's still a God who understands.

Song of Solomon

Author

Solomon (1:1), though some wonder if the song "of Solomon" is like the psalms "of David"—which could mean they are *by*, *for*, or *about* him.

Date

Solomon ruled around 970–930 BC.

In Ten Words or Less

Married love is a beautiful thing worth celebrating.

Details, Please

A dark-skinned beauty is marrying the king, and both are thrilled. "Behold, thou art fair, my love; behold, thou art fair; thou hast doves' eyes," he tells her (1:15). "Behold, thou art fair, my beloved, yea, pleasant: also our bed is green," she responds (1:16). Through eight chapters and 117 verses, the two lovers admire each other's physical beauty, expressing their love and devotion.

Quotable

Let him kiss me with the kisses of his mouth: for thy love is better than wine. (1:2)

He brought me to the banqueting house, and his banner over me was love. (2:4)

Many waters cannot quench love, neither can the floods drown it. (8:7)

Unique and Unusual

Like the book of Esther, Song of Solomon never mentions the name "God."

So What?

God made marriage for the husband and wife's enjoyment—and that marital love can be a picture of God's joy in His people.

ISAIAH

AUTHOR

Isaiah, son of Amoz (1:1).

DATE

Around 740–700 BC, starting "in the year that king Uzziah died" (6:1).

IN TEN WORDS OR LESS

A coming Messiah will save people from their sins.

DETAILS, PLEASE

Like most prophets, Isaiah announced the bad news of punishment for sin. But he also described a coming Messiah who would be "wounded for our transgressions. . .bruised for our iniquities. . .and with his stripes we are healed" (53:5). Called to the ministry through a stunning vision of God in heaven (chapter 6), Isaiah wrote a book that some call "the fifth Gospel" for its predictions of the birth, life, and death of Jesus Christ some seven hundred years later. These prophecies of redemption balance the depressing promises of God's discipline against Judah and Jerusalem, which were overrun by Babylonian armies about a century later. Isaiah's prophecy ends with a long section (chapters 40–66) describing God's restoration of Israel, His promised salvation, and His eternal kingdom.

QUOTABLE

Holy, holy, holy, is the LORD of hosts: the whole earth is full of his glory. (6:3)

Behold, a virgin shall conceive, and bear a son, and shall call his name Immanuel. (7:14)

For unto us a child is born, unto us a son is given: and the government shall be upon his shoulder: and his name shall be called Wonderful, Counsellor, The mighty God, The everlasting Father, The Prince of Peace. (9:6)

All we like sheep have gone astray; we have turned every one to his own way; and the LORD hath laid on him the iniquity of us all. (53:6)

UNIQUE AND UNUSUAL

Isaiah had two children with strange, prophetic names. Shear-jashub (7:3) means "a remnant shall return," and Maher-shalal-hash-baz (8:3) means "haste to the spoil." Shear-jashub's name carried God's promise that exiled Jews would one day return home. Maher-shalal-hash-baz's name assured the king of Judah that his country's enemies would be handled by Assyrian armies.

SO WHAT?

Early in His ministry, Jesus said He fulfilled the prophecies of Isaiah: "The LORD hath anointed me to preach good tidings unto the meek; he hath sent me to bind up the brokenhearted, to proclaim liberty to the captives, and the opening of the prison to them that are bound; to proclaim the acceptable year of the LORD" (61:1–2). It's amazing how much God cares about us!

JEREMIAH

AUTHOR

Jeremiah (1:1), with the assistance of Baruch, a scribe (36:4).

DATE

Approximately 585 BC.

IN TEN WORDS OR LESS

After years of sinful behavior, Judah will be punished.

DETAILS, PLEASE

Called to the ministry as a boy (1:6), Jeremiah prophesies bad news to Judah: "Lo, I will bring a nation upon you from far, O house of Israel, saith the LORD" (5:15). Jeremiah is mocked for his prophecies, occasionally beaten, and imprisoned in a muddy well (chapter 38). But his words come true with the Babylonian invasion of chapter 52.

QUOTABLE

Behold, as the clay is in the potter's hand, so are ye in mine hand, O house of Israel. (18:6)

UNIQUE AND UNUSUAL

The book of Jeremiah that we read is apparently an expanded, second version of a destroyed first draft. King Jehoiakim, angry with Jeremiah for his dire prophecies, cut the scroll with a penknife and "cast it into the fire that was on the hearth" (36:23). At God's command, Jeremiah produced a second scroll with additional material (36:32).

SO WHAT?

Through Jeremiah, God gave Judah some forty years to repent. God "is longsuffering to us-ward, not willing that any should perish, but that all should come to repentance" (2 Peter 3:9).

LAMENTATIONS

AUTHOR

Not stated but traditionally attributed to Jeremiah.

DATE

Probably around 586 BC, shortly after the fall of Jerusalem to the Babylonians.

IN TEN WORDS OR LESS

A despairing poem about the destruction of Jerusalem.

DETAILS, PLEASE

After warning the southern Jewish nation to obey God, the prophet Jeremiah witnesses the punishment he'd threatened. Judah's "enemies prosper; for the LORD hath afflicted her for the multitude of her transgressions," writes Jeremiah; "her children are gone into captivity before the enemy" (1:5). The sight brings tears to Jeremiah's eyes ("Mine eye runneth down with water," 1:16) and provides his nickname, "the weeping prophet." Lamentations ends with a plaintive cry: "Thou hast utterly rejected us; thou art very wroth against us" (5:22).

QUOTABLE

Turn thou us unto thee, O LORD, and we shall be turned; renew our days as of old. (5:21)

UNIQUE AND UNUSUAL

Though Lamentations doesn't indicate its author, Jeremiah is described in 2 Chronicles as a composer of laments (35:25).

SO WHAT?

God's punishment might seem severe, but as the book of Hebrews says, "No chastening for the present seemeth to be joyous, but grievous: nevertheless afterward it yieldeth the peaceable fruit of righteousness unto them which are exercised thereby" (12:11).

Ezekiel

Author

Ezekiel, a priest (1:1–3).

Date

Approximately the 590s–570s BC.

In Ten Words or Less

Though Israel is in exile, the nation will be restored.

Details, Please

Ezekiel, an exiled Jew in Babylon, becomes God's spokesman to fellow exiles. He shares unusual (even bizarre) visions with the people, reminding them of the sin that led to their captivity but also offering hope of national restoration.

Quotable

I have no pleasure in the death of him that dieth, saith the Lord GOD: wherefore turn yourselves, and live ye. (18:32)

Unique and Unusual

Ezekiel's vision of a valley of dry bones is one of the Bible's strangest images: "I prophesied as I was commanded: and. . .there was a noise, and behold a shaking, and the bones came together. . . .The sinews and the flesh came up upon them, and the skin covered them above. . . .And the breath came into them, and they lived, and stood up upon their feet, an exceeding great army" (37:7–8, 10).

So What?

Ezekiel strongly teaches personal responsibility: "The soul that sinneth, it shall die. But if a man be just, and do that which is lawful and right. . .he shall surely live" (18:4–5, 9).

DANIEL

AUTHOR

Likely Daniel, though some question this. Chapters 7–12 are written in the first person ("I Daniel," 7:15), though the first six chapters are in the third person ("Then Daniel answered," 2:14).

DATE

The period of the Babylonian captivity, approximately 605–538 BC.

IN TEN WORDS OR LESS

Faithful to God in a challenging setting, Daniel is blessed.

DETAILS, PLEASE

As a young man, Daniel—along with three others to be known as Shadrach, Meshach, and Abednego—are taken from their home in Jerusalem to serve the king of Babylon. Daniel's God-given ability to interpret dreams endears him to King Nebuchadnezzar, whose vision of a huge statue, Daniel says, represents existing and future kingdoms. Shadrach, Meshach, and Abednego find trouble when they disobey an order to bow before a statue of Nebuchadnezzar; as punishment, they are thrown into a fiery furnace, where they are protected by an angelic being "like the Son of God" (3:25). The next Babylonian king, Belshazzar, throws a drinking party using cups stolen from the temple in Jerusalem; he literally sees "the writing on the wall," which Daniel interprets as the soon-to-come takeover of Babylon by the Medes. The Median king, Darius, keeps Daniel as an adviser but is tricked into passing a law designed by other jealous officials to hurt Daniel, who ends up in a den of lions. Once again, God protects His people; Daniel spending a night and replaced by the schemers, who are mauled by the hungry beasts. The final six chapters contain Daniel's prophetic visions, including that of "seventy weeks" of the end times.

QUOTABLE

Our God whom we serve is able to deliver us from the burning fiery furnace, and he will deliver us out of thine hand, O king. (3:17)

My God hath sent his angel, and hath shut the lions' mouths, that they have not hurt me. (6:22)

O my God. . .we do not present our supplications before thee for our righteousnesses, but for thy great mercies. (9:18)

UNIQUE AND UNUSUAL

The book was originally written in two languages: Hebrew (the introduction and most of the prophecies, chapter 1 and chapters 8–12) and Aramaic (the stories of chapters 2–7).

SO WHAT?

As the old song says, "Dare to be a Daniel." God will always take care of the people who "dare to stand alone. . .to have a purpose firm" for Him.

Hosea

Author

Probably Hosea himself, though the text is in both the first and the third person.

Date

Sometime between 750 (approximately when Hosea began ministering) and 722 BC (when Assyria overran Israel).

In Ten Words or Less

Prophet's marriage to prostitute reflects God's relationship with Israel.

Details, Please

God gives Hosea a strange command: "Take unto thee a wife of whoredoms" (1:2). The marriage pictures God's relationship to Israel—an honorable, loving husband paired with an unfaithful wife. Hosea marries an adulteress named Gomer and starts a family with her. When Gomer returns to her life of sin, Hosea— again picturing God's faithfulness—buys her back from the slave market. The book contains God's warnings for disobedience but also His promises of blessing for repentance.

Quotable

For they [Israel] have sown the wind, and they shall reap the whirlwind. (8:7)

Unique and Unusual

Gomer had three children—perhaps Hosea's but maybe not—each given a prophetic name. Son Jezreel was named for a massacre, daughter Lo-ruhamah's name meant "not loved," and son Lo-ammi's name meant "not my people."

So What?

God is faithful, even when His people aren't—and He's always ready to forgive. "I will heal their backsliding," God said through Hosea; "I will love them freely" (14:4).

JOEL

AUTHOR

Joel, son of Pethuel (1:1). Little else is known about him.

DATE

Unclear but possibly just before the Babylonian invasion of Judah in 586 BC.

IN TEN WORDS OR LESS

Locust plague pictures God's judgment on His sinful people.

DETAILS, PLEASE

A devastating locust swarm invades the nation of Judah, but Joel indicates this natural disaster is nothing compared to the coming "great and very terrible" day of the Lord (2:11). God plans to judge His people for sin, but they still have time to repent. Obedience will bring both physical and spiritual renewal: "I will pour out my spirit upon all flesh," God says (2:28). When the Holy Spirit comes on Christian believers at Pentecost, the apostle Peter quotes this passage to explain what has happened (Acts 2:17).

QUOTABLE

Whosoever shall call on the name of the LORD shall be delivered. (2:32)

Multitudes, multitudes in the valley of decision: for the day of the LORD is near in the valley of decision. (3:14)

UNIQUE AND UNUSUAL

Unlike other prophets who condemned idolatry, injustice, or other specific sins of the Jewish people, Joel simply called for repentance without describing the sin committed.

SO WHAT?

Though God judges sin, He always offers a way out—in our time, through Jesus.

Amos

Author

Amos, a shepherd from Tekoa, near Bethlehem (1:1).

Date

Approximately the 760s BC.

In Ten Words or Less

Real religion isn't just ritual but treating people with justice.

Details, Please

An average guy—a lowly shepherd, actually—takes on the rich and powerful of Israelite society, condemning their idol worship, persecution of God's prophets, and cheating of the poor. Though God once rescued the people of Israel from slavery in Egypt, He is ready to send them into new bondage because of their sin. Amos sees visions that picture Israel's plight: a plumb line, indicating the people are not measuring up to God's standards, and a basket of ripe fruit, showing the nation is ripe for God's judgment.

Quotable

Prepare to meet thy God, O Israel. (4:12)

Seek good, and not evil, that ye may live. (5:14)

Let justice roll down as waters, and righteousness as a mighty stream. (5:24 ASV)

Unique and Unusual

A native of the southern Jewish kingdom of Judah, Amos was directed by God to prophesy in the northern Jewish nation of Israel.

So What?

How are you treating the people around you? In God's eyes, that's an indicator of your true spiritual condition. For a New Testament perspective, see James 2:14–18.

OBADIAH

AUTHOR

Obadiah (1:1), perhaps a person by that name or an unnamed prophet for whom "Obadiah" (meaning "servant of God") is a title.

DATE

Unclear but probably within thirty years after Babylon's invasion of Judah in 586 BC.

IN TEN WORDS OR LESS

Edom will suffer for participating in Jerusalem's destruction.

DETAILS, PLEASE

Edom was a nation descended from Esau—twin brother of Jacob, the patriarch of Israel. The baby boys had struggled in their mother's womb (Genesis 25:21–26), and their conflict had continued over the centuries. After Edom took part in the Babylonian ransacking of Jerusalem, Obadiah passed down God's judgment: "For thy violence against thy brother Jacob shame shall cover thee, and thou shalt be cut off for ever" (1:10).

QUOTABLE

Upon mount Zion shall be deliverance. (1:17)

UNIQUE AND UNUSUAL

Obadiah is the Old Testament's shortest book—only one chapter and 21 verses.

SO WHAT?

Obadiah shows God's faithfulness to His people. This prophecy is a fulfillment of God's promise from generations earlier: "I will bless them that bless thee, and curse him that curseth thee" (Genesis 12:3).

JONAH

AUTHOR

Unclear; the story is Jonah's but is written in the third person.

DATE

Approximately 760 BC. Jonah prophesied during the reign of Israel's King Jeroboam II (see 2 Kings 14:23–25), who ruled from about 793 to 753 BC.

IN TEN WORDS OR LESS

Reluctant prophet, running from God, is swallowed by giant fish.

DETAILS, PLEASE

God tells Jonah to preach repentance in Nineveh, capital of the brutal Assyrian Empire. Jonah disobeys, sailing in the opposite direction—toward a rendezvous with literary immortality. A storm rocks Jonah's ship, and he spends three days in a giant fish's belly before deciding to obey God after all. When Jonah preaches, Nineveh repents—and God spares the city from the destruction He'd threatened. But the prejudiced Jonah pouts. The story ends with God proclaiming his concern even for vicious pagans.

QUOTABLE

I will pay that that I have vowed. Salvation is of the LORD. (2:9)

Should not I spare Nineveh, that great city, wherein are more than sixscore thousand persons that cannot discern between their right hand and their left hand? (4:11)

UNIQUE AND UNUSUAL

Jonah's prophecy didn't come true—because of Nineveh's repentance.

SO WHAT?

God loves *everyone*—even the enemies of His chosen people. As Romans 5:8 says, "God commendeth his love toward us, in that, while we were yet sinners, Christ died for us."

MICAH

AUTHOR

"The word of the LORD that came to Micah the Morasthite" (1:1). Micah either wrote the prophecies or dictated them to another.

DATE

Approximately 700 BC.

IN TEN WORDS OR LESS

Israel and Judah will suffer for their idolatry and injustice.

DETAILS, PLEASE

Micah chastises both the northern and southern Jewish nations for pursuing false gods and cheating the poor. The two nations will be devastated by invaders (the Assyrians), but God will preserve "the remnant of Israel" (2:12).

QUOTABLE

He hath shewed thee, O man, what is good; and what doth the LORD require of thee, but to do justly, and to love mercy, and to walk humbly with thy God? (6:8)

UNIQUE AND UNUSUAL

Centuries before Jesus' birth, Micah predicted the town where it would occur: "But thou, Bethlehem Ephratah, though thou be little among the thousands of Judah, yet out of thee shall he come forth unto me that is to be ruler in Israel" (5:2).

SO WHAT?

Micah shows how God's judgment is tempered by mercy. "Who is a God like unto thee, that pardoneth iniquity, and passeth by the transgression of the remnant of his heritage? he retaineth not his anger for ever, because he delighteth in mercy" (7:18).

NAHUM

AUTHOR

"The book of the vision of Nahum the Elkoshite" (1:1). Nahum either wrote the prophecies or dictated them to another.

DATE

Sometime between 663 and 612 BC.

IN TEN WORDS OR LESS

Powerful, wicked Nineveh will fall before God's judgment.

DETAILS, PLEASE

"Woe to the bloody city!" Nahum cries (3:1). Nineveh, capital of the brutal Assyrian Empire, has been targeted for judgment by God Himself, who will "make thee vile, and will set thee as a gazingstock" (3:6) for sins of idolatry and cruelty. Nahum's prophecy comes true when the Babylonian Empire overruns Nineveh in 612 BC.

QUOTABLE

The LORD is slow to anger, and great in power, and will not at all acquit the wicked. (1:3)

The LORD is good, a strong hold in the day of trouble; and he knoweth them that trust in him. (1:7)

UNIQUE AND UNUSUAL

Nahum is a kind of Jonah, part 2. Though the city had once avoided God's judgment by taking Jonah's preaching to heart and repenting, now, more than a century later, it will experience the full consequence of its sins.

SO WHAT?

Even the most powerful city on earth is no match for God's strength. Neither is the biggest problem in our individual lives.

Habakkuk

Author

Habakkuk (1:1); nothing is known of his background.

Date

Approximately 600 BC.

In Ten Words or Less

Trust God even when He seems unresponsive or unfair.

Details, Please

In Judah, a prophet complains that God allows violence and injustice among His people. But Habakkuk is shocked to learn the Lord's plan for dealing with the problem: sending the "bitter and hasty" (1:6) Chaldeans to punish Judah. Habakkuk argues that the Chaldeans are far worse than the disobedient Jews, telling God, "Thou art of purer eyes than to behold evil" (1:13). The Lord, however, says He's only using the Chaldeans for His purposes and will in time punish them for their own sins. It's not Habakkuk's job to question God's ways: "The LORD is in his holy temple: let all the earth keep silence before him" (2:20). Habakkuk, like Job, ultimately submits to God's authority.

Quotable

The just shall live by his faith. (2:4)

I will joy in the God of my salvation. (3:18)

Unique and Unusual

The apostle Paul quotes Habakkuk 2:4 in his powerful gospel presentation in Romans 1.

So What?

Our world is much like Habakkuk's—full of violence and injustice—but God is still in control. Whether we sense it or not, He's working out His own purposes.

ZEPHANIAH

AUTHOR

Zephaniah (1:1).

DATE

Approximately 640–620 BC, during the reign of King Josiah (1:1).

IN TEN WORDS OR LESS

A coming "day of the Lord" promises heavy judgment.

DETAILS, PLEASE

Zephaniah begins with a jarring prophecy: "I will utterly consume all things from off the land," God declares in the book's second verse. People, animals, birds, and fish will all perish, victims of God's wrath over Judah's idolatry. Other nearby nations will be punished, as well, in "the fire of my jealousy" (3:8), but there is hope: In His mercy, God will one day restore a remnant of Israel that "shall not do iniquity, nor speak lies" (3:13).

QUOTABLE

The great day of the LORD is near. . .and hasteth greatly. (1:14)

The LORD thy God in the midst of thee is mighty; he will save, he will rejoice over thee with joy. (3:17)

UNIQUE AND UNUSUAL

Zephaniah gives more detail about himself than most of the minor prophets, identifying himself as a great-great-grandson of Hezekiah (1:1), probably the popular, godly king of Judah (2 Chronicles 29).

SO WHAT?

God gave the people of Judah fair warning of His judgment, just as He has done with us. For Christians, the coming "day of the Lord" carries no fear.

HAGGAI

AUTHOR

Haggai (1:1).

DATE

520 BC—a precise date because Haggai mentions "the second year of Darius the king" (1:1), which can be verified against Persian records.

IN TEN WORDS OR LESS

Jews returning from exile need to rebuild God's temple.

DETAILS, PLEASE

One of three "postexilic" prophets, Haggai encourages former Babylonian captives to restore the demolished temple in Jerusalem. The new world power, Persia, has allowed the people to return to Jerusalem, but they've become distracted with building their own comfortable homes. Through Haggai, God tells the people to rebuild the temple first in order to break a drought that's affecting the countryside.

QUOTABLE

Be strong, all ye people of the land, saith the LORD, and work: for I am with you, saith the LORD of hosts. (2:4)

UNIQUE AND UNUSUAL

Haggai seems to hint at the end-times tribulation and second coming of Christ when he quotes God as saying, "I will shake the heavens, and the earth, and the sea, and the dry land; and I will shake all nations, and the desire of all nations shall come" (2:6–7).

SO WHAT?

Priorities are important. When we put God first, He is more inclined to bless us.

ZECHARIAH

AUTHOR

Zechariah, son of Berechiah (1:1); some believe a second, unnamed writer contributed chapters 9–14.

DATE

Approximately 520–475 BC.

IN TEN WORDS OR LESS

Jewish exiles should rebuild their temple—and anticipate their Messiah.

DETAILS, PLEASE

Like Haggai, another postexilic prophet, Zechariah urges Jewish people to rebuild the Jerusalem temple. He also gives several prophecies of the coming Messiah, including an end-times vision of a final battle over Jerusalem, when "the LORD [shall] go forth, and fight against those nations. . . . And his feet shall stand in that day upon the mount of Olives. . . . And the LORD shall be king over all the earth" (14:3–4, 9).

QUOTABLE

Turn ye unto me, saith the LORD of hosts, and I will turn unto you. (1:3)

UNIQUE AND UNUSUAL

Zechariah's prophecy of the Messiah riding a donkey into Jerusalem (9:9) was fulfilled to the letter in Jesus' "triumphal entry" (Matthew 21:1–11). The prophecy "They shall look upon me whom they have pierced" (12:10) refers to the Roman soldiers' spearing of Christ after the crucifixion (John 19:34).

SO WHAT?

Knowing that many of Zechariah's specific prophecies were fulfilled in Jesus, we can trust that his other predictions—of the end times—will come true, too.

Malachi

Author

Malachi (1:1), meaning "my messenger." No other details are given.

Date

Approximately 450 BC.

In Ten Words or Less

The Jews have become careless in their attitude toward God.

Details, Please

Prophesying a century after the return from exile, Malachi chastises the Jews for offering "lame and sick" sacrifices (1:8); for divorcing their wives to marry pagan women (2:11, 14); and for failing to pay tithes for the temple (3:8). The Lord was angry with the attitude "It is vain to serve God" (3:14), but He promised to bless the obedient: "Unto you that fear my name shall the Sun of righteousness arise with healing in his wings" (4:2).

Quotable

Return unto me, and I will return unto you, saith the LORD of hosts. (3:7)

Unique and Unusual

Malachi, the last book of the Old Testament, contains the final word from God for some four hundred years, until the appearance of John the Baptist and Jesus, the Messiah, as prophesied in Malachi 3:1: "I will send my messenger, and he shall prepare the way before me, and the Lord, whom ye seek, shall suddenly come to his temple."

So What?

God doesn't want empty religious rituals—He wants people to worship Him "in spirit and in truth" (John 4:24).

MATTHEW

AUTHOR

Not stated but traditionally attributed to Matthew, a tax collector (9:9). Matthew is also known as "Levi" (Mark 2:14).

DATE

Approximately AD 70, when Romans destroyed the temple in Jerusalem.

IN TEN WORDS OR LESS

Jesus fulfills the Old Testament prophecies of a coming Messiah.

DETAILS, PLEASE

The first of the four *Gospels* (meaning "good news"), the book of Matthew ties what follows in the New Testament to what came before in the Old. The book, written primarily to a Jewish audience, uses numerous Old Testament references to prove that Jesus is the promised Messiah the Jews have been anticipating for centuries. Beginning with a genealogy that shows Jesus' ancestry through King David and the patriarch Abraham, Matthew then details the angelic announcement of Jesus' conception and the visit of the "wise men" with their gifts of gold, frankincense, and myrrh. Matthew introduces the character of John the Baptist, relative and forerunner of Jesus, and describes the calling of key disciples Peter, Andrew, James, and John. Jesus' teachings are emphasized, with long passages covering His Sermon on the Mount (chapters 5–7), including the Beatitudes ("Blessed are they. . .") and the Lord's Prayer ("Our Father, which art in heaven. . ."). As with all four Gospels, Matthew also details the death, burial, and resurrection of Jesus and is the only biographer of Jesus to mention several miracles—the tearing of the temple curtain, an earthquake, the breaking open of tombs, and the raising to life of dead saints— that occurred during that time (27:50–54).

QUOTABLE

She shall bring forth a son, and thou shalt call his name JESUS:

for he shall save his people from their sins. (1:21)

Ye are the salt of the earth. . . . Ye are the light of the world. (5:13–14)

Love your enemies, bless them that curse you, do good to them that hate you, and pray for them which despitefully use you, and persecute you. (5:44)

Judge not, that ye be not judged. (7:1)

Ask, and it shall be given you; seek, and ye shall find; knock, and it shall be opened unto you. (7:7)

Go ye therefore, and teach all nations, baptizing them in the name of the Father, and of the Son, and of the Holy Ghost. (28:19)

UNIQUE AND UNUSUAL

Matthew is the only Gospel to use the terms "church" and "kingdom of heaven."

SO WHAT?

As Messiah, Jesus is also King—and worthy of our worship.

MARK

AUTHOR

Not stated but traditionally attributed to John Mark, a missionary companion of Paul and Barnabas (Acts 12:25) and an associate of the apostle Peter (1 Peter 5:13).

DATE

Probably AD 60s, during the Roman persecution of Christians.

IN TEN WORDS OR LESS

Jesus is God's Son, a suffering servant of all people.

DETAILS, PLEASE

The second of the four Gospels is believed by most to be the first one written. The book of Mark is the briefest and most active of the four biographies of Jesus, the majority of which is repeated in the Gospels of Matthew and Luke. Mark addresses a Gentile audience, portraying Jesus as a man of action, divinely capable of healing the sick, controlling nature, and battling the powers of Satan. Mark's theme of the suffering servant comes through in his narratives of Jesus' interaction with hostile doubters—the Jewish leaders, who want to kill Him (9:31); His neighbors, who take offense at Him (6:3); and even His own family members, who think He's crazy (3:21). The abasement of Jesus pictures what His disciples should pursue: "Whosoever will be great among you, shall be your minister: and whosoever of you will be the chiefest, shall be servant of all. For even the Son of man came not to be ministered unto, but to minister, and to give his life a ransom for many" (10:43–45).

QUOTABLE

Come ye after me, and I will make you to become fishers of men. (1:17)

Suffer the little children to come unto me, and forbid them not: for of such is the kingdom of God. (10:14)

It is easier for a camel to go through the eye of a needle, than for a rich man to enter into the kingdom of God. (10:25)

Render to Caesar the things that are Caesar's, and to God the things that are God's. (12:17)

Watch ye and pray, lest ye enter into temptation. The spirit truly is ready, but the flesh is weak. (14:38)

UNIQUE AND UNUSUAL

Many believe an unnamed spectator at Jesus' arrest, mentioned in Mark's Gospel, was Mark himself: "And there followed him a certain young man, having a linen cloth cast about his naked body; and the young men laid hold on him: and he left the linen cloth, and fled from them naked" (14:51–52).

SO WHAT?

Suffering and loss aren't necessarily bad things—in fact, for Christians, they're the pathway to real life (8:35).

LUKE

AUTHOR

Not stated but traditionally attributed to Luke, a Gentile physician (Colossians 4:14) and a missionary companion of the apostle Paul (2 Timothy 4:11).

DATE

Possibly the AD 70s–80s, as the gospel was spreading throughout the Roman Empire.

IN TEN WORDS OR LESS

Jesus is Savior of all people, whether Jew or Gentile.

DETAILS, PLEASE

Luke's Gospel is addressed to a man named Theophilus (1:3), "to set forth in order a declaration of those things which are most surely believed among us" about Jesus Christ (1:1). It's unclear who Theophilus was, though some believe he may have been a Roman official—and Luke's book is the least Jewish and most universal of the four Gospels. Luke traces Jesus' genealogy beyond Abraham, the patriarch of the Jews, all the way back to Adam, "the son of God" (3:38), common ancestor of everyone. Luke also shows Jesus' compassion for all people: Roman soldiers (7:1–10), widows (7:11–17), the "sinful" (7:36–50), the chronically ill (8:43–48), lepers (17:11–19), and many others—including a criminal condemned to die on a cross beside Jesus (23:40–43). As with all the Gospels, Luke shows Jesus' resurrection, adding detailed accounts of His appearances to two believers on the Emmaus road and the remaining eleven disciples. As the Gospel ends, Jesus is ascending into heaven—setting the stage for a sequel of sorts, Luke's book of Acts.

QUOTABLE

For where your treasure is, there will your heart be also. (12:34)

I say unto you, that likewise joy shall be in heaven over one sinner that repenteth, more than over ninety and nine just persons, which need no repentance. (15:7)

Whosoever shall seek to save his life shall lose it; and whosoever shall lose his life shall preserve it. (17:33)

Whosoever shall not receive the kingdom of God as a little child shall in no wise enter therein. (18:17)

For the Son of man is come to seek and to save that which was lost. (19:10)

Unique and Unusual

Luke is the only Gospel to share Jesus' stories ("parables") of the good Samaritan (10:25–37), the prodigal son (15:11–32), and the rich man and Lazarus (16:19–31). Luke is also the only Gospel to detail Jesus' actual birth and words He spoke in childhood (both in chapter 2).

So What?

It doesn't matter who you are, where you come from, or what you've done—Jesus came to seek and to save you.

JOHN

AUTHOR

Not stated but traditionally attributed to John, the "disciple whom Jesus loved" (John 21:7), brother of James and son of Zebedee (Matthew 4:21).

DATE

Around the AD 90s, as the last Gospel written.

IN TEN WORDS OR LESS

Jesus is God Himself, the only Savior of the world.

DETAILS, PLEASE

While the books of Matthew, Mark, and Luke have many similarities (they're called the "synoptic Gospels," meaning they take a common view), the book of John stands alone. The fourth Gospel downplays Jesus' parables (none are recorded) and miracles (only seven are featured). Instead, John provides more extensive treatments of Jesus' reasons for coming to earth ("I am come that they might have life, and that they might have it more abundantly," 10:10); His intimate relationship with God the Father ("I and my Father are one," 10:30); and His own feelings toward the job He had come to do ("Father, the hour is come; glorify thy Son, that thy Son also may glorify thee: as thou hast given him power over all flesh, that he should give eternal life to as many as thou hast given him," 17:1–2). John also gives special emphasis to Jesus' patient treatment of the disciples Thomas, who doubted the resurrection (20:24–29), and Peter, who had denied the Lord (21:15–23).

QUOTABLE

In the beginning was the Word, and the Word was with God, and the Word was God. (1:1)

For God so loved the world, that he gave his only begotten Son, that whosoever believeth in him should not perish, but have everlasting life. (3:16)

I am the bread of life. (6:35)

I am the good shepherd: the good shepherd giveth his life for the sheep. (10:11)

I am the way, the truth, and the life: no man cometh unto the Father, but by me. (14:6)

Unique and Unusual

Jesus' very first miracle, His changing of water into wine at a wedding in Cana, is recorded only in John's Gospel (2:1–12). So is His raising of Lazarus from the dead (11:1–44), His healing of a man born blind (9:1–38), and His long-distance healing of a nobleman's son (4:46–54). John is also the only Gospel to mention Nicodemus, who heard Jesus' teaching that "ye must be born again" (3:7).

So What?

"These are written, that ye might believe that Jesus is the Christ, the Son of God; and that believing ye might have life through his name" (20:31).

ACTS

AUTHOR

Not stated but traditionally attributed to Luke, a Gentile physician (Colossians 4:14), a missionary companion of the apostle Paul (2 Timothy 4:11), and the author of the Gospel of Luke.

DATE

Covering events of the AD 30s–60s, Acts was probably written sometime between AD 62 and 80.

IN TEN WORDS OR LESS

The Holy Spirit's arrival heralds the beginning of Christian church.

DETAILS, PLEASE

Officially called "Acts of the Apostles," the book of Acts is a bridge between the story of Jesus in the Gospels and the life of the church in the letters that follow. Luke begins with Jesus' ascension into heaven after forty days of post-resurrection activity, "speaking of the things pertaining to the kingdom of God" (1:3). Ten days later, God sends the Holy Spirit on the festival day of Pentecost—and the church is born. Through the Spirit, the disciples are empowered to preach boldly about Jesus, and three thousand people become Christians that day. Jewish leaders, fearing the new movement called "this way" (9:2), begin persecuting believers, who scatter to other areas and spread the gospel through much of the known world. The ultimate persecutor, Saul, becomes a Christian himself after meeting the brightly shining, heavenly Jesus on the road to Damascus. Saul, later called Paul, ultimately joins Peter and other Christian leaders in preaching, working miracles, and strengthening the fledgling church.

QUOTABLE

Ye men of Galilee, why stand ye gazing up into heaven? this same Jesus, which is taken up from you into heaven, shall so come in like manner as ye have seen him go into heaven. (1:11)

Repent, and be baptized every one of you in the name of Jesus Christ for the remission of sins, and ye shall receive the gift of the Holy Ghost. (2:38)

Neither is there salvation in any other: for there is none other name under heaven given among men, whereby we must be saved. (4:12)

Saul, Saul, why persecutest thou me? (9:4)

Unique and Unusual

Acts tells of the first Christian martyr, Stephen, stoned to death for blaming Jewish leaders for the death of Jesus (chapter 7). Acts also depicts the gospel's transition from a purely Jewish message to one for all people (9:15; 10:45) and the beginning of the Christian missionary movement (chapter 13).

So What?

Christians today are driven by the same force that Acts describes: "Ye shall receive power, after that the Holy Ghost is come upon you" (1:8).

Romans

Author

The apostle Paul (1:1), with the secretarial assistance of Tertius (16:22).

Date

Approximately AD 57, near the conclusion of Paul's third missionary journey.

In Ten Words or Less

Sinners are saved only by faith in Jesus Christ.

Details, Please

Some call Romans a "theology textbook" for its thorough explanation of the Christian life. Paul begins by describing God's righteous anger against human sin (chapters 1–2), noting that everyone falls short of God's standard (3:23). But God Himself provides the only way to overcome that sin, "the righteousness of God which is by faith of Jesus Christ unto all and upon all them that believe" (3:22). Being justified (made right) through faith in Jesus, we can consider ourselves "to be dead indeed unto sin, but alive unto God through Jesus Christ our Lord" (6:11). God's Spirit will "quicken" (give life to, 8:11) all who believe in Jesus, allowing us to "present [our] bodies a living sacrifice, holy, acceptable unto God" (12:1). It is possible, with God's help, to "be not overcome of evil, but [to] overcome evil with good" (12:21).

Quotable

All have sinned, and come short of the glory of God. (3:23)

God commendeth his love toward us, in that, while we were yet sinners, Christ died for us. (5:8)

The wages of sin is death; but the gift of God is eternal life through Jesus Christ our Lord. (6:23)

O wretched man that I am! who shall deliver me from the body of this death? I thank God through Jesus Christ our Lord. (7:24–25)

We know that all things work together for good to them that love God, to them who are the called according to his purpose. (8:28)

Owe no man any thing, but to love one another: for he that loveth another hath fulfilled the law. (13:8)

Love worketh no ill to his neighbour: therefore love is the fulfilling of the law. (13:10)

UNIQUE AND UNUSUAL

Unlike Paul's other letters to churches, Romans was addressed to a congregation he'd never met. The great missionary was hoping to see the Roman Christians personally while traveling westward to Spain (15:23–24). It's unclear if Paul ever actually reached Spain or if he was executed in Rome after the end of the book of Acts.

SO WHAT?

In Paul's own words, "Therefore being justified by faith, we have peace with God through our Lord Jesus Christ" (5:1).

1 CORINTHIANS

AUTHOR

The apostle Paul, with the assistance of Sosthenes (1:1).

DATE

Approximately AD 55–57.

IN TEN WORDS OR LESS

An apostle tackles sin problems in the church at Corinth.

DETAILS, PLEASE

Paul had helped found the church in Corinth (Acts 18) but then moved on to other mission fields. While in Ephesus, he learns of serious problems in the Corinthian congregation and writes a long letter to address those issues. For those arguing over who should lead the church, Paul urges "that ye be perfectly joined together in the same mind and in the same judgment" (1:10). For a man involved in an immoral relationship with his stepmother, Paul commands, "Put away from among yourselves that wicked person" (5:13). For those church members filing lawsuits against others, Paul warns, "Know ye not that the unrighteous shall not inherit the kingdom of God?" (6:9). The apostle also teaches on marriage, Christian liberty, the Lord's Supper, spiritual gifts, and the resurrection of the dead. In the famous thirteenth chapter of 1 Corinthians, Paul describes the "more excellent way" (12:31): that of charity, or love.

QUOTABLE

For the preaching of the cross is to them that perish foolishness; but unto us which are saved it is the power of God. (1:18)

The foolishness of God is wiser than men; and the weakness of God is stronger than men. (1:25)

For other foundation can no man lay than that is laid, which is Jesus Christ. (3:11)

Take heed lest by any means this liberty of yours become a stumblingblock to them that are weak. (8:9)

I am made all things to all men, that I might by all means save some. (9:22)

For as often as ye eat this bread, and drink this cup, ye do shew the Lord's death till he come. (11:26)

Though I speak with the tongues of men and of angels, and have not charity, I am become as sounding brass, or a tinkling cymbal. (13:1)

Unique and Unusual

Refuting opponents who questioned his apostleship, Paul insists that he is as much an apostle as Jesus' original disciples. "Am I am not an apostle?" he asks in 1 Corinthians 9:1. "Have I not seen Jesus Christ our Lord?"

So What?

Church problems are nothing new—neither is the way to correct them. Personal purity, self-discipline, and love for others are vital to a congregation's success.

2 CORINTHIANS

AUTHOR

The apostle Paul, with Timothy's assistance (1:1).

DATE

Approximately AD 55–57, shortly after the writing of 1 Corinthians.

IN TEN WORDS OR LESS

Paul defends his ministry to the troubled Corinthian church.

DETAILS, PLEASE

Corinthian believers had apparently addressed some of the problems Paul's first letter mentioned—though there were still troublemakers who questioned his authority. He was forced to "speak foolishly" (11:21), boasting of hardships he'd faced serving Jesus: "in labours more abundant, in stripes above measure, in prisons more frequent, in deaths oft" (11:23). Paul even suffered a "thorn in the flesh" (12:7), which God refused to take away, telling him instead, "My grace is sufficient for thee: for my strength is made perfect in weakness" (12:9). His parting warning: "Examine yourselves, whether ye be in the faith; prove your own selves" (13:5).

QUOTABLE

For he hath made him to be sin for us, who knew no sin; that we might be made the righteousness of God in him. (5:21)

UNIQUE AND UNUSUAL

Paul never identifies his "thorn in the flesh," though some speculate it may have been bad eyesight, temptations, even physical unattractiveness.

SO WHAT?

Christians should respect authority—whether in the church, the home, or society at large.

GALATIANS

AUTHOR

The apostle Paul (1:1).

DATE

Perhaps around AD 49, as one of Paul's earliest letters.

IN TEN WORDS OR LESS

Christians are free from restrictive Jewish laws.

DETAILS, PLEASE

Writing to several regional churches, Paul can only "marvel" (1:6) that Galatian Christians have turned from their freedom in Jesus back to the rules of Old Testament Judaism. Some people tried to compel Christians "to live as do the Jews" (2:14), an error even the apostle Peter made (2:11–13). Paul argued strongly "that no man is justified by the law in the sight of God. . .for, The just shall live by faith" (3:11).

QUOTABLE

O foolish Galatians, who hath bewitched you? (3:1)

The fruit of the Spirit is love, joy, peace, longsuffering, gentleness, goodness, faith, meekness, temperance: against such there is no law. (5:22–23)

UNIQUE AND UNUSUAL

One of Paul's closing comments, "Ye see how large a letter I have written unto you with mine own hand" (6:11), makes some believe that poor eyesight was the apostle's "thorn in the flesh" (2 Corinthians 12:7).

SO WHAT?

Old Testament rules don't control Christians' lives—but God's Spirit should: "Walk in the Spirit, and ye shall not fulfil the lust of the flesh" (5:16).

EPHESIANS

AUTHOR

The apostle Paul (1:1).

DATE

Around AD 62, toward the end of Paul's life.

IN TEN WORDS OR LESS

Christians are all members of Jesus' "body," the church.

DETAILS, PLEASE

Paul had started the church in Ephesus (Acts 19) and now explains in detail the church members' relationship to Jesus Christ—so that they "may grow up into him in all things, which is the head, even Christ" (4:15). Through Jesus, God has reconciled both Jews and Gentiles to Himself (2:11–18). This new life should result in pure, honest living in the church and in the home (chapters 4–6).

QUOTABLE

By grace are ye saved through faith; and that not of yourselves: it is the gift of God: not of works, lest any man should boast. (2:8–9)

Put on the whole armour of God, that ye may be able to stand against the wiles of the devil. (6:11)

UNIQUE AND UNUSUAL

Paul tells servants (slaves, in today's language) to "be obedient to them that are your masters" (6:5). Why? Because God will reward such behavior (6:8).

SO WHAT?

"In him [Jesus] you too are being built together to become a dwelling in which God lives by his Spirit" (2:22 NIV).

Philippians

Author

The apostle Paul, along with Timothy (1:1).

Date

Probably the early 60s AD

In Ten Words or Less

"Friendship letter" between the apostle Paul and a beloved church.

Details, Please

With sixteen references to "joy" and "rejoicing," Philippians is one of the apostle Paul's most upbeat letters—even though he wrote it in "bonds" (1:13). Paul thanks the church at Philippi for its support (1:5) and encourages its people to "rejoice in the Lord alway: and again I say, Rejoice" (4:4).

Quotable

For to me to live is Christ, and to die is gain. (1:21)

I press toward the mark for the prize of the high calling of God in Christ Jesus. (3:14)

Be careful for nothing; but in every thing by prayer and supplication with thanksgiving let your requests be made known unto God. (4:6)

Unique and Unusual

Though unity is a common theme in Paul's letters, he singles out two Philippian women, Euodias and Syntyche, pleading that they "be of the same mind in the Lord" (4:2).

So What?

When we live in the joy of the Lord, "the peace of God, which passeth all understanding, shall keep your hearts and minds through Christ Jesus" (4:7).

COLOSSIANS

AUTHOR

The apostle Paul, along with Timothy (1:1).

DATE

Probably the early 60s AD

IN TEN WORDS OR LESS

Jesus Christ is supreme—over everyone and everything.

DETAILS, PLEASE

False teaching ("enticing words," 2:4) had infiltrated the church at Colosse, apparently causing some people to add unnecessary and unhelpful elements to their Christian faith. Paul sent this letter to remind Christians of the superiority of Jesus over Jewish rules and regulations (2:16), angels (2:18), and anything else. Jesus is "the image of the invisible God, the firstborn of every creature" (1:15).

QUOTABLE

For this cause we also, since the day we heard it, do not cease to pray for you. (1:9)

Set your affection on things above, not on things on the earth. (3:2)

Let the peace of God rule in your hearts, to the which also ye are called in one body; and be ye thankful. (3:15)

UNIQUE AND UNUSUAL

Paul mentions a letter to Laodicea (4:16) that apparently did not make the cut as New Testament scripture.

SO WHAT?

"Beware lest any man spoil you through philosophy and vain deceit, after the tradition of men. . .and not after Christ" (2:8).

1 Thessalonians

Author

The apostle Paul, along with Silvanus (Silas) and Timothy (1:1).

Date

The early 50s AD—perhaps Paul's earliest letter.

In Ten Words or Less

Jesus will return to gather His followers to Him.

Details, Please

In this letter to another church he helped found (see Acts 17), Paul teaches on the second coming of Christ, apparently an issue of some concern to the Thessalonians. Paul describes *how* Jesus will return but doesn't say exactly *when*. The important thing, in his words, is "that ye would walk worthy of God, who hath called you unto his kingdom and glory" (2:12).

Quotable

For the Lord himself shall descend from heaven with a shout, with the voice of the archangel, and with the trump of God: and the dead in Christ shall rise first. (4:16)

The day of the Lord so cometh as a thief in the night. (5:2)

Unique and Unusual

First Thessalonians contains two of the Bible's shortest verses: "Rejoice evermore" (5:16) and "Pray without ceasing" (5:17).

So What?

The Thessalonians were told to live right in view of Jesus' coming return. With the passage of two thousand years, don't you think it's more important for us today?

2 Thessalonians

Author

The apostle Paul, along with Silvanus (Silas) and Timothy (1:1).

Date

The early 50s AD—perhaps Paul's second-oldest letter.

In Ten Words or Less

Christians should work until Jesus returns.

Details, Please

Shortly after writing 1 Thessalonians, Paul dictates a follow-up. Apparently, a letter falsely claiming to be from Paul had left the Thessalonians "shaken in mind. . .troubled" (2:2) at the thought that Jesus had already returned. Paul assures them that the event is still future—and urges everyone to live positive and productive lives until the second coming. "If any would not work," Paul commands those who have dropped out in anticipation of Jesus' return, "neither should he eat" (3:10).

Quotable

You who are troubled rest with us, when the Lord Jesus shall be revealed from heaven with his mighty angels. (1:7)

Brethren, be not weary in well doing. (3:13)

Unique and Unusual

The fact that Paul dictated this letter is clear from his comment "The salutation of Paul with mine own hand. . .so I write" (3:17).

So What?

As with all of the Christian life, balance is key: We should always look forward to Jesus' return, but we should also be busy doing good while we're here on earth.

1 TIMOTHY

AUTHOR
The apostle Paul (1:1).

DATE
Approximately AD 63.

IN TEN WORDS OR LESS
Pastors are taught how to conduct their lives and churches.

DETAILS, PLEASE
The first of three "pastoral epistles," 1 Timothy contains the aging apostle Paul's insights for a new generation of church leaders. Timothy had often worked alongside Paul but was now pastoring in Ephesus (1:3). Paul warned him against legalism and false teaching (chapter 1), listed the qualifications for pastors and deacons (chapter 3), and described the behavior of a "good minister of Jesus Christ" (4:6) in the final three chapters.

QUOTABLE
Christ Jesus came into the world to save sinners; of whom I am chief. (1:15)

This is a true saying, If a man desire the office of a bishop, he desireth a good work. (3:1)

UNIQUE AND UNUSUAL
First Timothy seems to command good pay for pastors: "Let the elders that rule well be counted worthy of double honour. . . . The labourer is worthy of his reward" (5:17–18).

SO WHAT?
Though 1 Timothy is a letter to a pastor, Paul's teaching "that thou mayest know how thou oughtest to behave thyself in the house of God" (3:15) can speak to the rest of us, too.

2 TIMOTHY

AUTHOR

The apostle Paul (1:1).

DATE

Probably the mid-60s AD.

IN TEN WORDS OR LESS

The apostle Paul's final words to a beloved coworker.

DETAILS, PLEASE

Second Timothy may be the last known letter of Paul. Addressed to "Timothy, my dearly beloved son" (1:2), the book warns the young pastor against false teaching and urges him to live a life of purity before his congregation. Timothy should expect trouble ("All that will live godly in Christ Jesus shall suffer persecution," 3:12), but God will be faithful ("The Lord shall deliver me from every evil work, and will preserve me unto his heavenly kingdom," 4:18). Paul begs Timothy to join him as quickly as possible, as "the time of my departure is at hand" (4:6).

QUOTABLE

Thou therefore endure hardness, as a good soldier of Jesus Christ. (2:3)

UNIQUE AND UNUSUAL

Paul tells where the Bible comes from in 2 Timothy: "All scripture is given by inspiration of God" (3:16). The idea of the word *inspiration* is "breathed out."

SO WHAT?

We should all live life in such a way that we can say, like Paul, "I have fought a good fight, I have finished my course, I have kept the faith" (4:7).

TITUS

AUTHOR

The apostle Paul (1:1).

DATE

Approximately AD 63.

IN TEN WORDS OR LESS

Church leaders are instructed on their lives and teaching.

DETAILS, PLEASE

On the Mediterranean island of Crete, Paul left Titus to "set in order the things that are wanting, and ordain elders" (1:5) for the fledgling church. Known for their poor behavior (see "Unique and Unusual" below), the people of Crete needed the kind of church leader who holds fast to "the faithful word as he hath been taught, that he may be able by sound doctrine both to exhort and to convince the gainsayers" (1:9).

QUOTABLE

Not by works of righteousness which we have done, but according to his mercy he saved us, by the washing of regeneration, and renewing of the Holy Ghost. (3:5)

UNIQUE AND UNUSUAL

Paul quotes a Cretan philosopher in this letter: "One of themselves, even a prophet of their own, said, The Cretians are alway liars, evil beasts, slow bellies" (1:12). The quotation is from Epimenides, of the sixth century BC.

SO WHAT?

Though church leaders are held to a high standard, so are the people in the pews. What's good for the pastor is good for everyone else.

Philemon

Author

The apostle Paul (1:1).

Date

Probably around AD 63, when Paul was imprisoned in Rome.

In Ten Words or Less

Paul begs mercy for a runaway slave converted to Christianity.

Details, Please

Philemon is a "fellowlabourer" (1:1) of Paul, a man who has "refreshed" (1:7) other Christians with his love and generosity. But the apostle writes with a deeper request—that Philemon forgive and take back a runaway slave, who apparently accepted Christ under Paul's teaching: "my son Onesimus, whom I have begotten in my bonds" (1:10). "If thou count me therefore a partner," Paul wrote to Philemon, "receive him as myself" (1:17).

Quotable

I thank my God, making mention of thee always in my prayers, hearing of thy love and faith, which thou hast toward the Lord Jesus, and toward all saints. (1:4–5)

Having confidence in thy obedience I wrote unto thee, knowing that thou wilt also do more than I say. (1:21)

Unique and Unusual

With only one chapter and twenty-five verses, Philemon is the shortest of Paul's letters in the Bible.

So What?

Christians are called to forgive, and here's a practical example to consider. With God's help, will you let go of your grudges?

Hebrews

Author

Not stated; Paul, Luke, Barnabas, and Apollos have all been suggested.

Date

Probably sometime before AD 70, since Hebrews refers to temple sacrifices. The Jerusalem temple was destroyed by Romans in AD 70.

In Ten Words or Less

Jesus is better than any Old Testament person or sacrifice.

Details, Please

Written to Jewish Christians (hence the name "Hebrews"), this long letter emphasizes the superiority of Christianity to Old Testament Judaism. Jesus is "so much better" (1:4) than angels, Moses, and the previous animal sacrifices. "For if the blood of bulls and of goats, and the ashes of an heifer sprinkling the unclean, sanctifieth to the purifying of the flesh," Hebrews asks, "how much more shall the blood of Christ, who through the eternal Spirit offered himself without spot to God, purge your conscience from dead works to serve the living God?" (9:13–14). Jewish Christians, some of whom were apparently wavering in their commitment to Jesus, are reminded that Christ "is the mediator of a better covenant, which was established upon better promises" (8:6)—a once-for-all sacrifice on the cross that provides "eternal redemption for us" (9:12).

Quotable

How shall we escape, if we neglect so great salvation. (2:3)

There remaineth therefore a rest to the people of God. (4:9)

It is appointed unto men once to die, but after this the judgment. (9:27)

Not forsaking the assembling of ourselves together, as the manner of some is; but exhorting one another: and so much the more, as ye see the day approaching. (10:25)

Now faith is the substance of things hoped for, the evidence of things not seen. (11:1)

Wherefore seeing we also are compassed about with so great a cloud of witnesses, let us lay aside every weight, and the sin which doth so easily beset us, and let us run with patience the race that is set before us, looking unto Jesus the author and finisher of our faith. (12:1–2)

Let brotherly love continue. (13:1)

UNIQUE AND UNUSUAL

Hebrews is one of only two New Testament letters (the other being 1 John) that includes no greeting or hint of its author.

SO WHAT?

"Having therefore, brethren, boldness to enter into the holiest by the blood of Jesus. . .let us draw near with a true heart in full assurance of faith, having our hearts sprinkled from an evil conscience, and our bodies washed with pure water" (10:19, 22).

JAMES

AUTHOR

James (1:1), probably a brother of Jesus (see Matthew 13:55; Mark 6:3).

DATE

Approximately AD 60.

IN TEN WORDS OR LESS

Real Christian faith is shown by one's good works.

DETAILS, PLEASE

Though the apostle Paul clearly taught that salvation is by faith alone and not by good works (see Romans 3:28), James clarifies that good works will *follow* true faith: "What doth it profit, my brethren, though a man say he hath faith, and have not works?" (2:14). James encourages Christians, in everyday life, to view trials as opportunities for spiritual growth, to control their tongues, to make peace, to avoid favoritism, and to help the needy. The bottom line? "Therefore to him that knoweth to do good, and doeth it not, to him it is sin" (4:17).

QUOTABLE

Draw nigh to God, and he will draw nigh to you. (4:8)

The effectual fervent prayer of a righteous man availeth much. (5:16)

UNIQUE AND UNUSUAL

For those who think it's enough just to believe in God, James says, "The devils also believe, and tremble" (2:19). Life-changing faith in Jesus is the key.

SO WHAT?

Want practical wisdom for living the Christian life? You'll find it all through the book of James.

1 Peter

Author

The apostle Peter (1:1), with the assistance of Silvanus (Silas, 5:12).

Date

Approximately AD 65.

In Ten Words or Less

Suffering for the sake of Jesus is noble and good.

Details, Please

As the early church grows, the Roman Empire begins persecuting Christians—and Peter assures them that God is still in control: "Beloved, think it not strange concerning the fiery trial which is to try you, as though some strange thing happened unto you" (4:12). What is the proper response to such suffering? "Rejoice, inasmuch as ye are partakers of Christ's sufferings; that, when his glory shall be revealed, ye may be glad also with exceeding joy" (4:13).

Quotable

Be sober, be vigilant; because your adversary the devil, as a roaring lion, walketh about, seeking whom he may devour. (5:8)

Unique and Unusual

Peter clarifies exactly how many people rode out the great flood on Noah's ark: eight (3:20). Genesis indicates that "Noah. . .and his sons, and his wife, and his sons' wives" (Genesis 7:7) were in the boat but leaves unsaid whether any sons might have had multiple wives.

So What?

Life may be hard, but God is always good. And for Christians, there's a much better day ahead.

2 Peter

Author

The apostle Peter (1:1).

Date

Probably the late 60s AD, shortly before Peter's execution.

In Ten Words or Less

Beware of false teachers within the church.

Details, Please

The Christian qualities of faith, virtue, knowledge, self-control, patience, godliness, and love (1:5–8), coupled with a reliance on scripture (1:19–21), will help believers avoid the false teachings of those who "privily shall bring in damnable heresies, even denying the Lord that bought them" (2:1).

Quotable

We have not followed cunningly devised fables, when we made known unto you the power and coming of our Lord Jesus Christ, but were eyewitnesses of his majesty. (1:16)

The Lord is not slack concerning his promise, as some men count slackness; but is longsuffering to us-ward, not willing that any should perish, but that all should come to repentance. (3:9)

Unique and Unusual

Peter wrote this letter knowing his death was near: "Shortly I must put off this my tabernacle, even as our Lord Jesus Christ hath shewed me" (1:14).

So What?

"Beware lest ye also, being led away with the error of the wicked, fall from your own stedfastness" (3:17).

1 John

Author

Not stated but according to church tradition, the apostle John.

Date

Approximately AD 92.

In Ten Words or Less

Jesus was real man just as He is real God.

Details, Please

First John tackles a strange heresy that claimed Jesus had been on earth only in spirit, not in body: "Every spirit that confesseth not that Jesus Christ is come in the flesh is not of God: and this is that spirit of antichrist" (4:3). John wrote that he knew Jesus personally, as one "which we have looked upon, and our hands have handled" (1:1), and that knowledge leads to a saving belief in Jesus. Saving belief leads to obedience, but even when we sin, we know that God "is faithful and just to forgive us our sins" when we confess (1:9).

Quotable

Beloved, let us love one another: for love is of God. . . . God is love. (4:7–8)

Unique and Unusual

First John includes none of the usual features of a Bible letter—greetings, identification of the author, and the like. But it's a very warm, compassionate letter nonetheless.

So What?

"These things have I written. . .*that ye may know that ye have eternal life*" (5:13, emphasis added).

2 John

Author

The apostle John according to church tradition. The author is identified only as "the elder" (1:1).

Date

Approximately AD 92.

In Ten Words or Less

Beware false teachers who deny Jesus' physical life on earth.

Details, Please

Addressed to "the elect lady and her children" (1:1), perhaps an actual family or, figuratively, a church, 2 John tackles the heretical idea that Jesus had not been physically present on earth. The letter may be a reaction to the "gnostics," who taught that Jesus was spirit only and that He just appeared to suffer and die on the cross. This teaching, of "a deceiver and an antichrist" (1:7), should be avoided at all costs—to the point of barring one's door against those who believe it (1:10).

Quotable

I beseech thee, lady, not as though I wrote a new commandment unto thee, but that which we had from the beginning, that we love one another. (1:5)

This is love, that we walk after his commandments. (1:6)

Unique and Unusual

Second John, one of the New Testament's four single-chapter books, is the shortest by verse count: thirteen.

So What?

Just as in John's time, false teachers spread dangerous ideas in today's world. Every teaching should be weighed against scripture, 2 John says. "He that abideth in the doctrine of Christ, he hath both the Father and the Son" (1:9).

3 John

Author

The apostle John according to church tradition. The author is identified only as "the elder" (1:1).

Date

Approximately AD 92.

In Ten Words or Less

Church leaders must be humble, not proud.

Details, Please

Addressed to a believer named Gaius, 3 John praises those (like Gaius and another Christian named Demetrius) who lead in "charity before the church" (1:6). But 3 John also has harsh words for Christians like Diotrephes, "who loveth to have the preeminence" (1:9) and refuse to show kindness and hospitality to traveling evangelists.

Quotable

I have no greater joy than to hear that my children walk in truth. (1:4)

He that doeth good is of God: but he that doeth evil hath not seen God. (1:11)

Unique and Unusual

Third John, one of four single-chapter books in the New Testament, is the second shortest by verse count: fourteen.

So What?

Hospitality isn't just for the Martha Stewarts of the world—Christians are expected to feed, house, and encourage other believers, especially those who minister full-time for God. Humble service to others follows the example of Jesus Himself (see John 13:14).

JUDE

AUTHOR

Jude (1:1), possibly Jesus' half brother (see Matthew 13:55; Mark 6:3).

DATE

Approximately AD 82.

IN TEN WORDS OR LESS

Beware of heretical teachers and their dangerous doctrines.

DETAILS, PLEASE

Jude tackles the same problems Peter did in his second letter: false teachers who were leading the early church astray. "Murmurers" and "complainers" who were "walking after their own lusts" (1:16) were apparently using the grace of God as a cover for their sinful lifestyles—and encouraging Christian believers to do the same. True believers, Jude says, reflect God's love, show compassion, and work to pull sinners "out of the fire" (1:23).

QUOTABLE

Ye should earnestly contend for the faith which was once delivered unto the saints. (1:3)

UNIQUE AND UNUSUAL

Jude provides details of two Old Testament events not recorded in the Old Testament: the archangel Michael's fight with Satan over the body of Moses (1:9) and Enoch's prophecy of God's judgment (1:14–15).

SO WHAT?

Satan tries to sneak "secret agents" into God's church to confuse and ultimately crush true believers. It's the job of every true Christian to "earnestly contend for the faith" as passed down by Jesus' disciples and recorded in the Bible.

REVELATION

AUTHOR

John (1:1), probably the apostle.

DATE

Approximately AD 95.

IN TEN WORDS OR LESS

God will judge evil and reward His saints.

DETAILS, PLEASE

Jesus Christ Himself arranges for John to receive a "revelation" of "things which must shortly come to pass" (1:1). First, in chapters 2–3, Jesus gives John words of challenge and/or encouragement for seven churches—the good, the bad, and the in-between. Then the vision turns to the actual throne room of God, where a Lamb, looking "as it had been slain" (5:6), breaks seven seals from a scroll, unleashing war, famine, and other disasters on the earth. A dragon and two beasts, allied against God, arise to demand the worship of earth's people who have not been killed in the earlier catastrophes. The satanic forces and the people who follow them incur seven "vials of the wrath of God" (16:1), which bring plagues, darkness, and huge hailstones on earth. The upheaval destroys "Babylon the great," the evil and arrogant world system, just before an angel from heaven seizes Satan, "that old serpent" (20:2), and imprisons him for one thousand years. After a brief release to instigate a worldwide war, Satan is thrown into "the lake of fire and brimstone," where he will be "tormented day and night for ever and ever" (20:10). God unveils "a new heaven and a new earth" (21:1), where He will "wipe away all tears" (21:4) from His people's eyes.

QUOTABLE

Blessed is he that readeth, and they that hear the words of this prophecy, and keep those things which are written therein. (1:3)

Worthy is the Lamb that was slain to receive power, and riches, and wisdom, and strength, and honour, and glory, and blessing. (5:12)

Unique and Unusual

Revelation is an example of "apocalyptic literature," the only such book in the New Testament. *Apocalyptic* implies "revealing secret information." The book of Revelation identifies Jesus Christ as the "Alpha and Omega" (1:8) and reveals the number 666 as a sign of "the beast" (13:18).

So What?

"I've read the back of the book," an old Southern gospel song says, "and we win!" God has given His children a preview of how this world ends—and the new-and-improved world we'll enjoy forever. The curse of sin will be gone, we'll live in perfect fellowship with the Lord Himself, and we will "reign for ever and ever" (22:5). Kind of puts our bad days in perspective, doesn't it?

THE MOST IMPORTANT QUESTION ANYONE COULD ASK...

Who is Jesus?

For each of 66 names and attributes of Jesus,
Who Is Jesus? gives you a ten-word summary, a longer
description, a listing of key verses, a practical application,
and more. Patterned after the 2 million-copy bestseller
Know Your Bible—and written by the same author, Paul
Kent—*Who Is Jesus?* promises insight for believers and
seekers of any age or background. Small and easy-to-
read, it's packed with helpful information on Jesus—the
Alpha and Omega, Creator, Good Shepherd, and Word
Made Flesh, plus 62 other fascinating descriptions.

You'll get to know Jesus better. . .and deepen your
relationship with the most important Person of all time!

Paperback / 978-1-64352-247-0 / $2.99

Find This and More from Barbour Books
at Your Favorite Bookstore
www.barbourbooks.com